T0030836

LIA LEVI

JUST A GIRL

A TRUE STORY OF WORLD WAR II

Illustrations by
JESS MASON

Translated by
SYLVIA NOTINI

HARPER
An Imprint of HarperCollinsPublishers

Library of Congress Control Number: 2021949043
ISBN 978-0-06-306508-6

Typography by Laura Mock
23 24 25 26 27 LBC 8 7 6 5 4
❖
First U.S. Edition, 2022
Originally published in Italy in 2020 by HarperCollins Italia.

Twenty-five years after the publication of *Una bambina e basta*
by edizioni E/O, Lia Levi has adapted her story for young readers.

JUST A GIRL

1

ONE SUMMER AT THE SEASIDE

My name is Lia (if you look at the cover of this book, you'll find my name on it!) and I want to tell you the story of when I was a little girl. Mama, Papa, my two younger sisters, Gabriella and Vera, and I lived in a city in Italy called Turin.

Turin has a river and a park and lots of piaz-zas, which are like big town squares, but not the sea. It doesn't have the sea.

So when summer came, we would pack our bathing suits and our shovels and pails in our suitcases and take the train out to a tiny village with colored houses, sand, beach umbrellas, and small blue waves you could wade into even if you didn't know how to swim.

That's why my story starts with a newspaper stand right on the beach and my parents telling six-year-old Lia, "Today, you're going to buy the newspaper."

As I said, the stand is right at the end of the beach, which means you don't have to cross the road to get there. It is not dangerous for children.

Hmm. Why are they telling me to go buy a newspaper right now?

I think about it for a while. Then I understand.

I just finished first grade, but it is as if I never set foot in my classroom. As if I didn't even sit at those ugly desks, doing what everyone else did.

The reason is easy to explain. I was terribly (*terribly!*) shy, and at school I couldn't get one single sound to come out of my mouth.

Do you know what a baby bird sounds like? *Peep . . . peep . . . peep*? That was my voice. No one could hear it.

During my first days, the teacher listened extra hard, trying to understand what I was saying, but soon she got bored, preferring to just let the other children speak.

So when my parents send me to buy the newspaper, this is what they want: they want to make me do things that will force me to talk to other people!

So now I'm standing in front of the newsstand holding tightly to a coin.

"Sir, sir!" I think I'm shouting to the big man behind the counter.

But all that's coming out is probably the usual *peep . . . peep . . . peep*. And he isn't turning around.

How can I possibly get a newspaper? If I'm still holding this coin when I get back to my parents on the beach, they are going to be very unhappy.

That's when I make a very smart decision. I reach up and place the coin on the counter and

take the newspaper myself.

"Here it is!" I yell, waving the newspaper. (When I'm with my parents I *do* have a voice.)

Papa happily takes it, but then asks, "Where's the change?"

"The man didn't give me any," I whimper. Which is actually the truth.

This story does not end well.

The three of us—me, Papa, and Mama—head to the newsstand, where the man says he didn't see any money and tells us to pay for the newspaper I took.

It's a lie, but Papa pays anyway because he doesn't like to argue.

2

BYE-BYE, SCHOOL

The next day Mama tells me she wants to have a talk with me.

Oy vey! She wants to talk about the newspaper again, I think, annoyed.

But it's not that. Mama makes me sit down and tells me in a very serious tone of voice, "You won't be able to go back to school this year."

Why is she making such a sad face? I'm so happy! I can go right ahead talking in my *peep peep peep* voice, and there won't be anyone around to get angry.

But I'm afraid this will upset my mama, so I ask, "Why can't I go anymore?"

"Mussolini doesn't want Jewish children in Italian schools," she says.

That's silly! Who would ever believe something so ridiculous?

I know perfectly well that being *Jewish* means:

1. Going to synagogue some Saturdays (every Saturday would be too much).

2. Lighting two candles on Friday evenings (but Mama takes care of that) and one each night for Hanukkah (which also means getting gifts).

3. Fasting for a day once a year—that is, eating nothing (but this doesn't apply to children).

4. Not eating bread for eight days at Passover, only 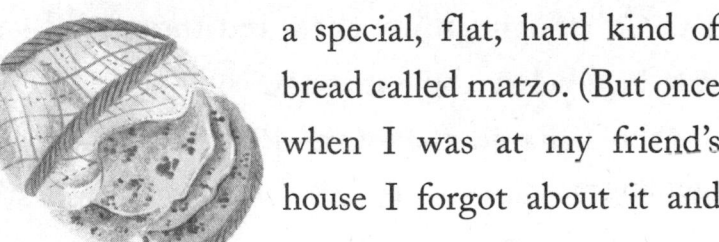 a special, flat, hard kind of bread called matzo. (But once when I was at my friend's house I forgot about it and

devoured a roll with butter and jam.)

And there's another thing I know too.

Mussolini is our leader. He is in charge of everybody. And in class, in the songs and poems that we recite all together, we call him "Duce! Duce!"

So why would our leader even care if certain Jewish children (only certain ones) are not doing very well in school just because they are extra shy?

I really think Mama is confused, so I run to Papa.

I explain all these things I've been thinking about, but he doesn't smile at all. Actually, his face is even more serious than Mama's.

"Remember when you broke the blue glass vase and then said it was your sister Vera who'd knocked it over?"

What does that vase have to do with this? Now I sit up straight in my chair and turn red. I was sure he'd believed me that day.

"You behaved that way," Papa continues very calmly, "because your sister was small and still couldn't speak very well, so she couldn't defend herself. And because you knew that we would never have been angry with her."

Help! This is all I need after what happened with the newspaper!

But, luckily, it seems Papa isn't planning to scold me.

"I want you to understand that sometimes blaming someone else is also a way of keeping people quiet. For example, are there some things that don't work very well in a country? Sure! So the leaders of the country find people who are different from them—maybe because they believe in another religion—and they say, 'It's *their* fault! *They're* our enemies.' People believe them, and they're even happy because then they know who to be angry with."

I stay quiet for a long time. Papa's words are hard to understand. I need to think them over. Then I say to him, "Are you saying that Mussolini is doing this with the Jews?"

Papa nods. That's when I shout, "That's a horrible thing to do! I'll never chant 'Duce! Duce!' again!"

I am sure Papa will like my answer, but he doesn't. He even seems angry. He grabs me by the shoulders, or maybe he's just hugging me.

"Listen carefully," he tells me. "The Duce decides everything by himself, and everyone else has to say yes to him. Anyone who speaks out against him ends up in prison."

I must look really scared, because my papa quickly adds, "Not children, but they might arrest their parents."

How does that keep a child from worrying?

Papa must guess what I'm thinking because he starts being funny and patting me on the shoulder, and we laugh a little bit.

"Promise me just one thing," he says. "Never tell anyone what I've just explained to you."

Do I even have to promise that?

Everyone knows my voice: *peep . . . peep . . . peep . . .*

Nothing happens for the next two days. Luckily, nobody wants to talk to me.

My sisters and I like to build sandcastles, even though Vera is too little. But she won't leave us alone, and wants to do whatever we do, so Mama always makes us let her play.

One afternoon there's a contest called *BUILD A SANDCASTLE!* We run off to the beach quickly so Vera can't catch us. A sister *that* little would make us lose for sure.

Then I see Mama and Papa running toward me, looking very happy.

"You don't need to stop going to school!" they

shout together. "In Turin, close to the synagogue, they're organizing a Jewish school. You'll go there!"

What a nice way to spoil my day at the beach!

I thought that by freeing me from school, at least Mussolini had done one good thing for me.

3

JEWISH SCHOOL

My cousin Annarosa goes to the Jewish school. She is only a year ahead of me, but she thinks she's a lot older.

When she sees me at her school, she decides she'll be my protector from now on. Good luck to anyone who plays a trick on me or, worse, anyone who tries to give me a penalty for losing a game. They'll have to deal with her.

"My cousin is little," Annarosa snarls, and pulls me toward her.

I really am small. Even worse, I have round cheeks that look like two small apples, and my mama always ties a red ribbon on my head that makes me look like a butterfly.

In the end there's no one who doesn't obey my cousin, and when it comes time to decide who has to play the donkey during recess, all the other children point at me and yell, "Not her!" Sometimes they even give me a colored pencil or a few pages from a comic book.

In the classroom, when the teacher, Maestra Ginetta, hears the *peep . . . peep . . . peep* that comes out of my mouth, she smiles at me. Maybe she has little children at home like me.

Passover is here (the holiday that lasts eight days and you can only eat matzo, remember?).

The first night we all sit around the biggest table ever. Before eating, even if dinner is ready, we first read aloud, one part each from a book, the story of how Moses helped the Jews escape from Egypt many years ago. There was a very bad man in charge there, called Pharaoh, who beat them if they didn't do what he wanted.

Our family always went to our grandparents' house to hear the story about Moses read aloud, but since Nonno Reuven died, we don't go there anymore.

The Jewish school makes the Passover dinner with the book and everything. Mama says, "This year we're going to the Jewish school," and I'm happy because my cousin Annarosa will be there too.

The principal tells us that many more people than usual decided to come to the school dinner this year. I wonder why.

So there we are sitting around a narrow but very long table, and it feels like everyone is looking at me. It's because Mama did something very nice. Instead of a red ribbon, she made me a bow with two ribbons for my hair: one white, the other light blue, just like the colors of the Jewish flag.

I'm sure, though, that what happens later has nothing to do with those blue and white ribbons.

But wait a minute! First I have to explain another thing about Passover—when we read from the book about Moses and his adventures, the smallest child at the table has to ask *the four questions*.

The first question is: "Why is tonight different from all other nights?" (The other questions are more or less the same.) But it's all pretend; we already know the answers. It's only so that a grown-up can start to tell the story over again. It's a kind of game, like a school play.

But for the child chosen to ask those famous questions, it isn't a game at all. The child's parents take two months, sometimes four, to make him or her learn all the words they will have to say.

And do you know what happens this time?

The teacher, Maestra Ginetta, quietly walks over to our table and stops. She takes *me* by the hand and drags me gently around the room.

Where are we going? I wonder, more than a little scared.

We walk all the way to the middle table, the

one where the rabbi is seated—he's like a priest for Catholics.

Maestra Ginetta makes me stand on a chair.

"Now you will recite the four questions," she whispers, smiling.

"But I don't know them!" Now I'm even more scared. The time my cousin Arnaldo, whom I don't like, recited the questions, I wasn't listening.

"Don't worry," the teacher says quietly. "I'll give you a cue, a little at a time."

And that's exactly how it goes.

As she softly sings the words in my ear, I repeat them so that the others can hear them too.

I'm so worried right now that I'm not thinking about anything else, so I don't realize (I really don't) that as I'm singing, my voice is getting louder.

By the fourth question, I'm like a singer belting from the stage with my arms open wide.

When it's all over, I get down from the chair, and everyone rushes over to squeeze my hand and hug me. "Well done! Very well done!" they say.

When Mama and Papa come over, I can see they're almost crying.

"Your voice . . . your voice," Papa stammers. I really don't understand why he's acting so strange.

"Didn't you notice?" Mama asks me. "Your voice could be heard even in the farthest corners of the room."

No, I hadn't noticed. I thought that all I was

supposed to do was *lend* my voice to such a kind teacher.

And if you really want to know, I'll tell you. Yes! The voice I *lent* to Maestra Ginetta stayed that way *forever*.

4

PAPA "LOSES" HIS JOB

When I was really little, I lost my teddy bear at the beach. His name was Nerino, even though he was all white and only his eyes were black. I loved Nerino. I left him under the beach umbrella late one afternoon, and the next morning he was gone.

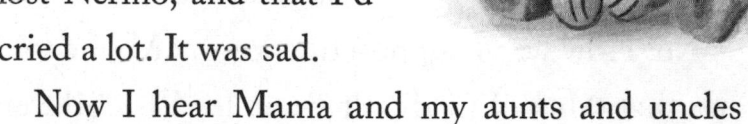

Everyone knew I'd lost Nerino, and that I'd cried a lot. It was sad.

Now I hear Mama and my aunts and uncles

saying ever so quietly that Papa has *lost* his job.

I can't understand this. You can't forget a job late one afternoon under a beach umbrella.

Papa no longer goes to his office in the morning.

I don't know why he's decided not to. It seems to me he'll get bored staying home, but maybe he's decided to be a painter. He sits there all day with a large canvas, brushes, and colors, and you know what he wants to paint? Me. He wants to paint *my* portrait, with the frame and all the rest, which is usually what happens to a queen.

I don't like sitting there without moving. After a while, my neck hurts too.

One day I jump up and snort, "Papa, why don't you go back to the office?"

Papa makes a sad face and Mama gets very angry with me.

She drags me off to another room and says, "They sent him away, just like they sent you away from your school! Don't you understand?"

No. How was I supposed to know? Mama told me that Mussolini didn't want Jewish children in Italian schools anymore, but my papa isn't a Jewish child, and he hasn't gone to school for ages.

Why would Mussolini want to get rid of some poor workers who spend the whole day in an office, some days without even a break? Maybe he's even more evil than I thought.

Then I think of another thing. They opened a Jewish school for Jewish children, so maybe they

would be able to invent a "Jewish job" for Jewish fathers.

"Is Papa sad that he can't go to his office anymore?" I ask Mama somewhat hesitantly.

And guess what she answers?

"When you work, at the end of each month they give you money so you can pay for everything your family needs. If you don't work, they give you nothing."

That really scares me. I remember all those stories they tell in books, the ones where there is a child who is so poor he doesn't even have a few coins to buy himself a tiny piece of cake.

Mama realizes I'm feeling scared, and she gives me a hug.

"We have some savings in the bank," she says. "We'll use that money."

I don't know what savings are, but one day Papa takes me to the bank with him. There's a counter there and some kind gentlemen give you all the money you ask for. This makes me feel better.

But it doesn't always work that way. Mama

didn't tell me because she wanted to make me feel better. I found out about it later.

Those *savings* run out after a while. And those kind gentlemen give you *absolutely nothing* after that.

5

BOOM! BOOM! THE WAR IS HERE

There was already a war. Even the children knew this.

On one side there were the Germans (commanded by a very bad man named Hitler, who hated Jews even more than Mussolini did), and on the other side there were the French, the British, and others, who had joined the war to make the bad people lose.

Not Italy, though. It preferred to stay out of the war and watch, and all the Italians seemed happier that way.

But if you don't join in and play the game, you'll never win.

Mussolini must have thought about it, and do you know who he chose as a teammate for this war? Hitler, the one who hated Jews more than anything else in the world.

Mama and Papa, my aunts and uncles, grandparents, cousins, and my teachers from the Jewish school, and so many other people whom we didn't know, became very sad. They were so sad they didn't even have the strength to get angry anymore.

But in the meantime, the war had come to our house, and I'm going to tell you how.

It is summer, and one late afternoon we are still at the public gardens in Piazza Carlo Felice with our nanny.

You haven't met our nanny yet. Her name is Maria, and she came to stay with us when I was born. For us children she has always been a part of the family, like an aunt, the kind that spends their whole life yelling at you. That's what old aunts do: they love you, but they're always criticizing everything.

This evening my sisters and I are at the public gardens with Maria. Mama and Papa are away. They left by train to look for a house in the country for the holidays, because the one that we are so fond of at the seaside is too expensive. Banks don't give you money to rent a house at the seaside.

We are playing quietly in the garden, and we aren't even arguing. Then all of a sudden Maria says, "Everyone stand up and keep still. We have to listen to Mussolini's speech."

Mussolini isn't actually there, but we can hear his voice booming all around us because there are speakers hidden in the trees.

"People of Italy, do you want war?" Mussolini shouts.

And wherever his voice is coming from, all we can hear around him is, "We do! We do!" being shouted out even louder.

Then there are other words, but I stop listening because I am getting bored. I do hear the last word he says, which is "*victory*."

Maria takes us by the hand and says, "Let's hurry home."

But before I go on with my story, I need to explain something very important.

One of the countries at war was France.

And France is very close to the city of Turin. Getting there by plane is the shortest trip you'll ever take.

Everyone in Italy was thinking, *Today, at six p.m. we're going to declare war, and tomorrow we begin fighting!*

But no. Three hours later, the French planes flew over us with their buzzing sound, and they started to bomb Turin.

We're sleeping, my sister Gabriella and me, in our bedroom. Vera is sleeping in the small bed that has been moved to Maria's room.

All of a sudden, we hear a terrible explosion! It sounds to me like the night, and I really mean the *night*, is shattering into a thousand pieces, like a toy thrown out of a window by some naughty child.

And then there are explosions everywhere, the lights go out, turn back on for a moment, but go out again. And far away in the distance, a siren is wailing.

"Maria! Maria!" we cry out, scared to death.

Maria runs into the room right away, already holding our little sister in her arms.

Ever so quietly, we try to open the shutters. A policeman is running in his pajamas, wearing only the hat from his uniform. "Hurry! Head to the shelters!" he cries out.

Head to the shelters? What does that mean?

We all turn to look at Maria. But she doesn't know either.

In the distance we can see thousands of fires on the city roofs.

Maria quickly closes the shutters. Then she puts all three of us in Mama and Papa's big bed.

"There's no need to be afraid," she says after a while. "It's just fireworks. They're pretending. They're just practicing for the war."

But every time we hear another explosion, we start crying. And each time we cry, Maria tells us in an almost cheerful voice, "They're pretending! They're pretending!"

When everything is really over and it's quiet again, my sisters fall fast asleep.

But not me.

And that's why I hear the phone ring. I know right away that Nonna Giorgina is on the other end of the line.

"Oh, signora! Oh, signora!" the nanny says to her, and I can tell that Nonna is crying.

"It's just pretend! It's just pretend!" she told us.

But I didn't believe her for a single second. Luckily for us, nothing terrible happens that night.

Mama and Papa rush back the next morning.

"But why? But why? Couldn't you all have gone down into the shelter?" they say to Maria. I can tell they are a little angry.

"I don't even know where the shelter is!" she tells them. She sounds even angrier than they are.

That same evening, we learn exactly where the shelter is.

This time the alarm sounds first, and this time the war is for real. All three of us girls, together with Mama, Papa, and Maria, rush down the stairs wearing jackets over our pajamas.

Surprise!

The "shelter" is the basement underneath the house, where we keep the sacks of coal for the boiler and where, sometimes, we are allowed to store wine flasks and empty suitcases. All that fuss for something so easy, and almost silly. Couldn't they have just told us it was the basement?

Down here, along with all the parents and grandparents, are all the children who live in the building. There are enough of us to start a game.

But above us we hear that horrible *boom! boom!* every now and then . . . so it's better to sit still and not say a word.

6

THE FOG IN MILAN

Now I'm in third grade in the Jewish school, and I have to admit that (now that I have a voice) I'm feeling pretty happy.

But one day Mama and Papa tell me that our money in the bank is about to run out. Papa absolutely must find a job.

I know he's looked and looked but hasn't found anything.

Not only did Mussolini fire all the Jews from the office, he also told everyone: "No one is allowed to give them jobs anywhere else."

Papa looks at me. I'm scared again, and he

explains that his hope is to find a secret job. Not a job in a big office with a lot of people, but in a tiny one, where one man who works by himself lets someone help him but without anyone knowing.

And that's exactly what happens! This is the news my Papa was waiting for. We all dance around the table with joy.

But there is one thing he didn't tell me.

The job isn't in Turin, it's in another city: Milan.

How can that be?

Here in Turin, we have Nonna Giorgina and Nonna Teresa (who's not Jewish, though), my cousin Annarosa and her family, and Maestra Ginetta, who treats me as if I were her youngest daughter.

What's more, here in Turin we have:

1. The longest and largest river in all of Italy.
2. A huge park to play in.
3. A pointed church steeple that you can see in all the postcards.

We know nothing about Milan, and we don't know anyone there.

School! That's what comes to my mind, besides Maestra Ginetta.

"Papa," I tell him very seriously, "I have to go to the Jewish school."

"But of course!" Mama cries out happily. "You'll finish third grade here and have a much bigger Jewish school for fourth grade in Milan."

We leave before the fall, and Maria comes with us. She's our nanny, and she would never be someone else's nanny just to stay in Turin.

We live in a house close to a park and go to a new Jewish school. (My sister Gabriella is in second grade. Vera doesn't go to school yet.)

But something very strange happens. In the school in Milan they all say, "Lia comes from Turin. She's in fourth grade. She's very smart!"

I will never know where this piece of news, which is false, came from. In Turin I was pretty good at writing essays, but when I did math, my brain would always fall asleep.

Is it because of the four questions at Passover when I was in second grade? But that was because the teacher helped me!

Nonna Teresa used to always play this trick on me. She'd say, "What a nice girl you are," and then she would ask me to do her a favor. I'm only telling you that to explain why things go the way they do at the Jewish school in Milan.

Everyone *thinks* I am smart, so I *become* smart.

I write whatever I think of, and lots of the things I write are things I imagine. In Turin they used to tell me that I could only write things that are true. But here in Milan, the more I use my imagination, the happier the teacher is!

I feel like a bird whose wings have grown stronger so it can fly better.

In Milan, the fog hides everything. Sometimes when we walk to school, Maria and I can't stop laughing because we're not sure where we are. We're surrounded by a cloud. Our hands and legs are tickled by a thousand pinpricks.

Milan really is a loving city. It gathers everyone in a pillow of feathers, and it squeezes them in a big, big hug.

In cafés where the light streams in through every window, children can order whipped cream that comes in a cup and a spoon made of very hard chocolate. After you finish the whipped cream, you can eat everything else, including the cup and the spoon. It's like taking a giant step closer to happiness.

One day my mama calls me (again) to one side.

There has been a mistake. Or maybe not—maybe something's changed.

Papa's job in Milan has fallen through.

"Don't be afraid." Mama tries to smile. "The job

is still there, but we have to move to Rome."

To Rome?

Rome is a very faraway city. When I told you we didn't know anyone in Milan, it wasn't true. We found some relatives there right away.

But Rome, no way! We really, *really* don't know anyone there. It will be like traveling to a foreign country.

"Are we leaving as soon as the school year is over?" I sigh with great sadness.

"We're leaving at the end of the month." Mama sighs too.

"What about school?" I cry.

"You'll finish fourth grade at the Jewish school in Rome."

"No way!" I cry out even louder and run away.

I don't slam my bedroom door that day, but for the rest of my life Mama and Papa will remind me of that day and say I did.

7

THE SKYSCRAPER IN ROME

Papa leaves before we do. He has to find us a house. Six people (three of whom are children) can't just show up in another city and start walking around lugging their suitcases.

When we get to Rome, Papa is waiting for us at the station and tells all of us to get into a taxi. The taxi has a long way to go, and it seems we just keep going and going.

"There it is!" Papa finally cries out, leaning out the window and pointing.

It's a very tall house that goes all the way up to the sky. The house is there all by itself, with no other buildings nearby. There's a grassy lawn at the bottom and the windows are green, too, like the lawn, and guess what the name of the neighborhood is? *Monteverde!* Which means "green mountain."

I'll tell you everything about the neighborhood right away. Over the years other new buildings will go up around that house. An open square and lots of streets will be built too. But not yet. Now, there is nothing else there.

The tall house sits there alone, and everyone calls it the skyscraper.

When you go inside, there's a big foyer with a narrow counter for Signor Amedeo, the doorman, and to either side, on both the right and the left, there are two stairways that go all the way up to the ninth floor.

We live on the fifth floor, and what do we discover?

On the sixth floor, right above our heads, lives a Jewish family with lots of children, and living at the top of the other staircase is none other than the

headmistress of the Jewish school and her family. (But we won't find this out until later.)

This kind of situation is completely new to us. The only Jews we were familiar with before this were our own relatives.

This time going to a new school is not going to be easy.

The school year is already half over, and in Rome it seems like everyone has studied something different. Some kids are ahead, and other kids are behind.

"That's not how we do division," they tell me. "No writing down what you're subtracting. We do everything in our heads." And for history? "Were you asleep at your school in Milan? How can you possibly be so far behind?"

Most of all they make fun of my Piedmontese accent, or maybe it's that I use all the correct verb tenses and all the matching adjectives—being an excellent student from the North of Italy.

They think I'm a show-off and imitate me

behind my back, walking around holding their heads up straight—the way (according to them) countesses do.

The Jewish school in Rome is big, much bigger than the ones in Turin and Milan combined.

Some of the children come from the small streets in the old Jewish quarter, where they've been used to going around anywhere they like and shouting without anyone telling them what to do. So there's always lots of confusion at school. Sometimes they get into fights with each other, and the teachers and janitors have to rush over and split them up.

At first, I am afraid when these things happen, but I get used to it. Nothing bad ever comes of it anyway. Actually, all you hear is laughter in the hallways.

It feels as if my other schools were in black and white and this one is in color.

When we arrive in the morning we don't go straight to the classroom. We go into a big hall, and each class huddles around its teacher. The teachers look like mama hens with their chicks following behind.

Then things become orderly: we all line up in twos while the music teacher starts playing a march on the piano.

"Off we go to the vast blue sea," we sing, stomping our feet, as we file toward our classroom.

The line is made up of a boy and a girl, one next to the other, one wearing a white uniform, the other wearing a blue one, from youngest to oldest. I hold hands with my neighbor because that's how we did things in the North. I was taught good manners. I know nothing yet about real life and what other people think.

My neighbor is turning all red and puffy. I can tell he's trying to pull himself together and be polite back, but behind us it is complete chaos. I don't notice it too much, but the other kids are laughing and making jokes. They're kicking and elbowing each other and throwing themselves on the ground pretending to trip. They roll their eyes and fake hug each other.

I continue not to pay too much attention.

A few months later, when I have only started to catch on, the other children trap us in the classroom by ourselves during recess and say we're engaged.

Locked in the classroom, this time I cry.

This is the first and last time I will ever be fooled at this school.

My sisters and I have friends who live in the same neighborhood, and they go to the Jewish school too. One of them is in my class. Her name is Fiorella.

Our parents liked each other right away, and now as we head down the hill to the school, which is close to the river, our fathers walk side by side.

While they talk, we girls start talking too—telling each other our secrets and forming a bond with one another. It's sort of like when you mix flour, water, and the other ingredients, and knead everything well, to make dough for bread.

That's how Fiorella became my best friend.

At the Jewish school in Rome, Mussolini is ever present. When I hear the things they say about him, I stare in surprise. A long time ago my papa explained to me that what was happening to us Jews was all Mussolini's fault. But he made me promise I would never tell anyone. It would be dangerous. But now, at this school, everyone is making fun of Mussolini, and the teachers are the first ones to do it. In math class, children write a pun on the blackboard. It's a safe way to say "Down with the Duce!"

The teacher pretends she's angry, but actually she's quite pleased.

In the classroom, like in every school, we're supposed to stand as we listen to the war bulletin on the radio. The war bulletin tells you what's happening in the places where Italy is fighting the war. The voice we hear the most often says: "Our troops have attested to positions that are more favorable."

None of us really understands what the voice means by that. Could *attested* mean that soldiers have to take school tests while fighting?

Nope. The teacher calmly explains to us that all those words mean is simply that the fascist soldiers have had to withdraw.

We clap our hands and jump up on our desks. If the bad guys are losing, that must mean the good guys are winning, right?

8

NONNA TERESA'S SURPRISE

By now we know all about the laws against the Jews (no school, no papas allowed to go to work, et cetera, et cetera).

There are other laws, too, but who wants to even think about them?

Mama and Papa pretend everything is fine.

But there is one law that could still give us a lot of trouble: it says that Jews can't go on vacation. Not to the seaside or to anywhere else, for that matter.

No one can explain why.

But that law—too bad for *them*—doesn't work on *us*!

We have a grandma, Nonna Teresa, who isn't Jewish. She can very easily rent an apartment right near the beach in the village with the colorful little houses where we always went on vacation. And if she invites her two granddaughters, no one will notice.

And so that summer, right after I finished fourth grade, Mama and Papa decide that my sister Gabriella and I will go to stay with our nonna Teresa and her housekeeper, Cesarina, in the village by the seaside.

Our younger sister, Vera, is too little to come. She will stay in Rome with Mama and Papa, so they can spoil her as much as they want without having to listen to us complain.

Three months at Nonna Teresa's without our parents! Gabriella isn't sure she wants to go, afraid that she might get sad sometimes at night and feel like crying.

Not me!

Nonna Teresa is different from my mama. She

enjoys seeing us eat and thinking up weird things to feed us.

As soon as we arrive, she takes us to the scale at the pharmacy and weighs us. She will weigh us again before we leave. More than anything she wants to fatten us up. She even has the hairdresser cut our hair, so our faces look rounder.

Cesarina has us taste her eggplant parmesan. No one has ever cooked it at our house! And every evening, *every single evening,* she makes a different kind of dessert for us. Truth be told, Cesarina is more of a cook than a housekeeper. She invents a new recipe every day.

One day Nonna surprises us and brings us out to the rocks overlooking the pier to have dinner. Cesarina comes, too, carrying a big basket.

In the distance a red sun is setting over the water, and in front of us appears a long plate (it looks like it was made of silver) filled with Russian potato salad.

"Oooh!" my sister and I say in amazement at the same time, our mouths wide open like two eggs.

It's the most fabulous, most unforgettable dinner I have ever had in my whole life.

Sometimes Nonna tells us things she makes up, then she forgets and tells us something completely different. If we say something about it to her, she laughs.

One day she explains it to us like this: a real lie is one thing—like the lies you tell to defend yourself when you've been naughty—but it's another thing to tell a good lie, which you only tell for fun. They're called *inventions*, and poets and fairy-tale writers use them too.

Nonna Teresa really likes complicated situations.

One evening she decides she will take me to the

outdoor movies. But only *me*. My sister is too little. Nonna tells me to get in bed fully dressed, and when Gabriella falls asleep, Nonna pulls me out from my sheets and drags me happily all the way to the movies. Going at night is even more fantastic than going at daytime and makes me dream a lot after.

But the next day my sister finds out, I don't know how, and she starts crying and screaming.

To calm her down, Nonna promises she will take Gabriella to see a movie another night, and this time all four of us go, Cesarina too.

Mama would not be at all pleased with so much chaos, and that's why when I write to her I don't tell her about our "secret" trips to the movies.

I just said that I wrote to Mama, but I don't actually write letters.

Before leaving Rome, my mama reminded me: "We're going to be apart for three months, and there are too many things I'm not going to know about what you're doing." So she asked me to keep a diary, to write something small in it every day. That way, when we get back, she will be able to know everything about our vacation at Nonna's. I am very diligent, and each day I write down what happened.

But I don't write down any of Nonna's amusing inventions, or any of my secret thoughts—especially not those.

9

NANNY MARIA

Help! This time we can't pretend that nothing is wrong.

Sometimes balloons can be fun. But sometimes you blow one up and *boom!* it pops right in your face and scares you, because you weren't expecting it to break.

We thought we had gotten used to all the anti-Jewish laws. We fooled everyone with Nonna Teresa, so we figured we knew what we were doing.

But no.

Now it's Maria.

The law says that a "Christian" (in other words, someone who is not Jewish) is not allowed to work for a Jewish family.

We already knew that.

But we are the only Jewish family allowed to have a Christian nanny, and there is a reason for that. Papa explains it to me with a word that is really hard to pronounce.

Discriminate.

To discriminate can mean to treat someone badly because of something that's different about them. But Papa says discriminate can also mean treating someone better because they have some advantage. For example, you might get treated better when you get an A+ at school. So discriminating can work against you or in your favor.

In our family, the advantage is this: Papa is the son of an officer who died fighting for Italy in the war before this one.

Papa, poor thing, was just a boy, so he became a "war orphan." It's very sad, but it also makes people respect him.

And that "discrimination" (which was stamped in capital letters on the papers they gave us) granted us special privileges. But now someone says no more.

A police officer came to our house and took away our radio, saying, "It's not allowed," because there was a new law saying Jews can't have a radio in the house.

Before, if you insisted a little, they would bring it back. But not anymore.

Then the same thing happens with Maria.

This time the police officer's face becomes more serious as he tells us our nanny has to leave. She cannot stay in a house with Jews.

Sometimes Maria can be grumpy, and she's always grumbling about something, but she's part of our family. Without her we will wobble, like a table that's missing a leg.

We always think that Vera is too little to understand what's going on. But this time she's the first to understand that something is wrong.

She grabs Maria's skirt and starts to cry.

Then all of us are crying, and Maria is hugging us, calling us "my girls."

Then Mama has an idea. We could ask our neighbor living on the same landing as us if she will pretend that Maria is working for her. Maria would sleep there; she could even help them wash the dinner dishes or do other things. But the rest of the time, she would stay with us like before, and, of course, our family would continue to pay her salary.

Our neighbor is pleased with the idea and says yes. Now Maria will be with us forever.

Hurrah! We are so happy.

But things never seem to work out the way you hope they will.

Little by little, Maria gets used to the other house. Whenever we go over there to see her, she pushes us right out, saying, "There are guests here. I'm very busy."

She always has a million things to do that keep her from coming over: closets to straighten out, the little boy has a fever, the lady of the house wants

Maria to fix her hair.

Maria is even beginning to *look* like the other house. It gets to the point that she thinks she's doing us a favor by crossing the landing to come over to our house. And when she does come over, she tells us stories about the other family that we are not at all interested in.

One evening we keep ringing the doorbell. We ring and ring. We need to ask *our* nanny something.

Finally, she opens the door just a little. She is wearing an elegant black uniform and a lacy white apron.

"We have an important guest. I think he's a mayor," she whispers quickly to us. "Go away. I have lots to do."

She shoves us out and shuts the door.

Maria, what are you doing? Are you throwing us out? We changed schools. Papa lost his job (even though he found another one). We left the city where we grew up. But you? You're Maria. Maria the Grump. You're part of our family. You can't just disappear like this from our lives.

I keep all these sad thoughts inside, but then enough is enough. Life goes on.

Maria still comes to our house almost every day, usually with a frown on her face.

Anyway, we have plenty of other things to do.

Another year in Rome has come and gone, and I have my fifth-grade exam to study for—and my admission test for middle school! For that I need my picture taken for a document like the ones adults have; otherwise they won't even let you take the exam.

10

MUSSOLINI'S GONE
(BUT IT'S ONLY A TRICK)

It's July and it's hot.

We won't be taking a vacation at Nonna Teresa's this summer. Papa says the war is getting too close. The Americans have landed with their ships in Sicily, he tells us, and Sicily—as we learned in school—is the biggest island in Italy.

In other words, the Americans are already in our country, and soon they're going to reach us too. Then there will be no more bad laws, especially the ones against Jews.

I forgot to tell you that at a certain point America entered the war on the good guys' side. (Everyone says America instead of the United States to make things easier.) That's when everything was supposed to get better.

America is very big. It has huge factories that can manufacture up to eight (yes, I said eight!) huge ships a day. They used those ships to sail all the way to Sicily.

And that's why everyone thinks that the good guys are going to win in the end.

One night in July, the three of us are already in bed, because it's late.

Suddenly, we hear lots of noise coming from inside our very own house. And the same commotion of loud, disorderly voices is coming through the windows that open onto the street too.

"Mama!" I shout, trying to sound annoyed. "You woke us up!"

Now what would you expect to hear from a mother who forces you to "turn out the lights and don't make a sound" at nine o'clock every night? Wouldn't you expect her to say, "I'm sorry, girls.

We didn't realize we were making so much noise"?

But instead, Mama, followed by Papa, and by the people who live in our building whom we hardly know, come into our room dancing. Each is holding a glass in their hand and singing, "Fascism has fallen! Mussolini's gone!"

Then Mama lifts her glass up to the ceiling as if making a toast.

Papa explains calmly that the Italians couldn't stand the Duce anymore—or the war, a war that he was making the whole country lose. So the king, who is even more in charge than Mussolini, has chased him out.

"The fascist laws will no longer be enforced, and the ones against the Jews even less so," Papa adds, with a very pleased look on his face.

Does this mean we can be happy now?

I'm not so sure. It looks to me like people are half cheerful and half worried.

Finally, I understand why.

Mussolini is gone, *but the war is still here.*

And which side are we fighting on? The bad

guys' side! The side of the Duce's pals! Even though we just threw him out!

Not even the greatest adventure writer could have invented such a mess.

My dearest readers and (I hope!) friends, All I'm doing is telling you the story of when I was a little girl, and I don't want to make it sound too complicated.

I'm sorry if it is! It's not my fault that history is so disorderly.

First of all, I need to tell you something important. In the war that I'm telling you about, the Germans were the bad guys. But you must not think that being German makes someone a "bad guy." Like all the people in the world, there are kind and very kind Germans, and bad and very bad Germans. At the time of our story, the German soldiers were under the orders of the very evil Hitler, and they willingly carried out the bad things they were ordered to do.

Luckily, what happened back then is just a bad memory now.

Here's some information that will help you understand what happened to me and to my family:

1. Italy changed sides in the war without even telling its allies first (namely, the Germans).
2. This made the Germans so angry, they occupied Italy with their troops. Now, on the streets, all you could hear was the *clunk! clunk!* of their jackboots.

For us Jews, it got much, much worse.

In the other countries occupied by the Germans, the Jews were all arrested and taken who knows where.

But for the Jews in Rome—where the pope lived (he was the head of all the churches)—maybe there was hope, because if the German soldiers (with their jackboots) started doing bad things right in front of him, then he would see it with his own eyes. Maybe he would do something about it. Now people began expecting to hear good news.

◦ ◦ ◦

The Germans gather all the Jewish leaders in Rome and tell them, "We won't lay a finger on any of you who live in this city if you give us fifty kilos of gold."

Fifty kilos! That's a lot of gold! Over 110 pounds!

Everyone scrambles to get whatever gold they have at home and bring it to some large room near the synagogue where it will be collected.

We rummage through all our drawers and take all the gold chains (with the Star of David) our nonna gave us when we were born. Mama finds a small bracelet too. She even tries to remove the gold clasp on a velvet handbag (even though Papa doubts very much that it is really made of gold).

Our family doesn't bring much, but somehow— I don't know how—together, we make it to fifty kilos.

Hurrah! We're safe!

Don't believe it, though, because that's not how things go. . . .

11

THE PLAN

Mama wants to talk to me again.

She has the same face from that day a long time ago at the beach. Whatever she wanted to tell me that day didn't seem so serious.

But this time I'm a little afraid.

I'm eleven now, so I can see what's happening and understand better.

"The pope is in Rome," Mama tells me.

Oy vey! I already know that. Does she really need to repeat it?

"So the Jews aren't in danger. We gave our gold to the Germans."

This was another thing I'd heard her say a million times.

"So?" I ask, looking straight into her eyes.

Mama says that yes, everything is fine, but that parents need to be very, very careful. And in fact, they have come up with a plan.

Mama and the headmistress at the Jewish school went and talked to some nuns who live in a convent at the edge of the city near the countryside.

And so?

So these nuns agreed to take in her daughters as well as the headmistress's daughters at the boarding school, my mama explained hastily.

Boarding school? I know what a boarding school is. It's like a school, except that the students eat and sleep there. In other words, they *live* there.

"But why do we need to stay at a boarding school?" I murmur, my voice trembling slightly.

Papa must have been right behind the door because suddenly he is in the bedroom with us.

"You're the eldest and you need to know exactly how things stand," he says to me in a serious voice.

It's best to hide, he explained, because with the Germans around it's not safe. And we need to follow all the safety rules.

The nuns said (and my parents agree) that we must never say we are Jewish, that we should go by a false last name (the Germans know all the Jewish last names because they have written them all down), and that we should be able to recite Christian prayers like the other girls in the boarding school.

"But I don't know any Christian prayers!" I holler, because in all that confusion it's the first thing I can think of.

"You'll have to learn them," Mama retorts briskly.

There's something else I want to explain to you, dear readers. Don't think poorly of my mama. When it comes to saving one's children, mothers (and fathers) have no higher priority. They have no time for minor details.

Papa is smarter at convincing me.

"You've read lots of books about heroic children who become secret agents and manage to save themselves from a thousand dangerous situations," he reminds me. "Try to imagine yourself as one of those characters."

Well, I definitely like this idea more. But then I think about something else. "What about you? Where will you be?"

Mama and Papa answer in unison, saying that if one day there really is any danger, two adults will be able to escape in a flash if they don't have to take any children with them.

It's still September, but it's raining as though the sun has taken a long vacation.

We're on a bus headed to a convent in the countryside with Mama, the school headmistress, and her two children. Maria is with us too. She's come back to help our family.

As soon as we arrive, the nuns bring us to a big room with lots of beds lined up. In the back of the room, enclosed by a white curtain, is where the nuns sleep. After we put down our suitcases, the nuns take us to explore the classrooms, the dining hall, and lots of small rooms each with a piano—where anyone can take music lessons.

I say I want to, but Mama says nothing.

The tour has ended.

"Say goodbye to your mama," the nun, whose name is Sister Maria Luisa, says gently.

What does she mean by *say goodbye to your mama?*

I quiver.

"Where are you going?" I cry.

Of course, I know the answer. They have already explained to me that we girls will have to stay hidden here by ourselves.

But you understand, don't you? My mind refuses to pass the message on to my heart.

And *say goodbye to your mama* are words my heart simply can't grasp.

12

ONE MORNING IN OCTOBER

When we arrive at the convent, I am promoted to my second year of middle school; my sister Gabriella is promoted to fifth grade. Vera is supposed to begin first grade this year, but she screams and hollers, "No! No!" so loudly that the nuns get worried and decide to let her stay in kindergarten for another year. When they tell Mama, she doesn't seem to mind.

Living at a boarding school is not a good thing. But it's not a bad thing, either. This is what's bad about boarding school:

1. You no longer have your own house. At home,

you can scream up and down the hallway and no one says, "Be quiet!" In boarding school, you can't do that.

2. In the afternoons, at home, if you've finished your homework, you can get up and leave. You're free. Not at boarding school. There's homework time, but you have to stay seated at your desk until the bell rings, even if you've finished. And what do you do until then? You twiddle your thumbs.

3. When homework time is over, we all go into a huge hall to recite the rosary. That's a Christian prayer where one person talks and another person answers. When we're finished with that, we can finally go and play.

4. Getting used to a fake name is hard. At the beginning, you have to be very careful because you're not used to it, and when someone calls it out, you don't even turn around. Luckily, our fake name sounds a lot like our real one. The real one is Levi, the false one is Lenti. Pretty clever, don't you think?

5. And of course: Mama and Papa. We see them only on Sundays when they come to visit.

This is what's good about a boarding school:

1. There are lots of girls here. At home, sometimes on rainy days, you can't find a friend to play with. At boarding school there are lots of girls to choose from (but you have to choose the right ones, because some of them aren't so nice).

2. There's a real stage with a red velvet curtain that opens and closes. In a room behind the stage, there are baskets of all sizes filled with beautiful costumes. There's even a costume with a cloak— for dressing up like a lady from olden times. My

sisters and I have always done plays, but only for school recitals, or on our parents' balconies, and the costumes were just colored paper.

3. I take piano lessons now, and soon I'll be able to play "Twinkle, Twinkle, Little Star" from beginning to end.

I guess I was joking about what's good and bad about boarding school. Everyone knows that almost any kid would rather be home.

School in here is the same as school out there. Attendance, oral pop quizzes, homework . . . it's not much fun at all.

One morning in October, I'm in class.

Carlotta, the girl sitting next to me, is watching the rain beating down on the windows. Suddenly, she stands up. I don't know why.

"Hey," she whispers to me. "Your mama's outside, in the courtyard."

My mama? At this time of day? Why didn't they call me?

"May I go now?" I ask the nun who's teaching.

"My mama is downstairs."

"You can go downstairs later, when the lesson's finished," Sister Maria Speranza answers in a strict tone of voice.

"But why *later*? My mother is here now."

"She'll be here *later* too," Sister Maria Speranza states, and instead of looking at me, she too stares out the window at the falling rain.

As soon as the bell rings, I race down the stairs, leaving all my books behind on my desk.

"Mama!" I cry out, bursting into the headmistress's office. "Why didn't you tell someone to come and get me?"

"There's no rush," Mama whispers. "I think I'll be here for a while." And then she turns to look at Sister Giacinta, the elderly and wise Mother Superior at the school.

Sister Giacinta opens her arms wide. It must be her way of saying *who knows*.

I didn't even notice, but the headmistress of the Jewish school is there with my mama too.

Both of them glance at each other, then Mama blurts out, "The Germans! The Germans!" She is almost in tears. "This morning they started taking away the Jews! We only managed to escape because we were warned in time, but the others . . . They took almost everyone who was living in the Jewish quarter. . . ."

Now Mama really is crying.

I can't move. I feel like my arms and legs are made of stone.

I'm finding it hard to understand, and inside me it's as if fire and ice are fighting one against the other.

How is this possible? You said that if we gave the Germans our gold chains, nothing bad would happen to us in Rome.

"They tricked us," Mama mutters. "We believed the Germans' promises. How could we possibly have imagined this?"

Suddenly, I remember something else.

"Papa!" I cry out. "Where's Papa?"

"I don't know," Mama answers. "We split up. I came here because the nuns have a boarding house at the other end of the park." She explains that she's asked them if she can stay here. Now she is waiting for their answer. "Papa told me that he would find us somewhere to stay," she adds, forcing herself to smile.

But she must see on my face that I am still very scared.

"Don't worry," she whispers. "He'll know how to hide. He's like you—he loves books about secret agents who always manage to escape danger."

Dear readers, this might not seem like the right moment to say this, because certain things happened later, and I will have to tell you about them further on.

But I don't want you to worry.

So I'm going to tell you in advance: what Mama said was quite true.

Papa lived in several boarding houses in the city, under a false name, pretending that everything was fine. But in each place, as soon as one of the other boarders became curious and asked too many questions, he would pack up his bags and go somewhere else.

When we all went back home, he showed us a notebook where he drew the funny faces of the people he had met.

Remember how, when he lost his job, he started painting?

Well, after that he became a painter forever.

13

WINTER WITH THE NUNS

At the boarding school everything is different now.

Mama wasn't the only one to come knocking at the convent door.

Suddenly, lots and lots of new girls arrived, hair messy and so frightened. They were dragged here without even a suitcase by parents who were even more frightened. They had all been living peacefully in their homes when the Germans started searching for Jews to take away.

But these girls and their parents managed to escape in time. Just like Mama and Papa.

Now that they're here, the nuns have moved us all to a much larger room.

Before, five of us were Jews. Now there are more than thirty of us hiding at the school.

I know most of the new girls. A few months ago, we were all together in the main hall of the Jewish school in Rome, where the music teacher played the march on the piano and we all filed out and headed to our classrooms. Now I can see they're afraid, that they don't know where anything is here. Some of them are laughing nervously, and their little sisters are crying just like mine does. They look in wonder at the five of us who were already here.

I need to tell you something.

Sometimes some of us are a little bit naughty.

I know everything there is to know about life at the boarding school, and I also know how to avoid getting in trouble with the nuns. For instance, I know that even if you have finished your homework, you need permission to leave your seat and walk around, and that it's forbidden to chat in the dormitory after the light is switched off.

Since I'm the oldest of the Jewish group, the new girls need my help. They're always asking me questions.

And sometimes I act like a snob. I answer their questions like a know-it-all, and sometimes the tone I use is rude.

Many years later I'll think back to this and regret it.

But in the evening, when we all gather in the boarding school dormitory, we move close to each other, and with the nuns' permission, we recite the

Jewish prayer together: "Hear, oh Israel, the Lord is our God . . . the Lord is One."

In boarding school it's best if you behave yourself.

At the end of every week we assemble in the main hall, with the Mother Superior and sometimes the abbess (who is even more important than the Mother Superior), and they give out awards for good behavior.

If you've behaved well, they place a pink sash over your shoulder. If you did well at school that week, you get a blue one instead.

Being awarded both sashes is the greatest possible achievement, but no one has ever succeeded in doing that (and anyway, two sashes are too many). Mama says the blue one is worth more because it means you've worked hard at your studies.

Besides those of us who live here, there are "outsiders" in our classes too. These are students who only come for the lessons and return home afterward. We're at war (we get that), and the buses are hardly running because there's a gas shortage. So when lessons end each day, Sister Emerenziana gathers all the non-boarders in a group and walks them home.

Every day I grasp her arm and won't let go.

"And what do you want?" she says lightheartedly. "Have you forgotten that you live here?"

"I want to keep you company, so that you don't have to walk back by yourself," I murmur.

She looks at me.

"You want to go and walk past the gate, don't you, Lia?" she whispers in my ear. "You're not a prisoner here. The park is very big. You can run all the way up to the fields, as far as where the fields begin if you like."

I shake my head. What do I care about the park?

"I want to see the streets and the shops and everything else," I tell her.

"You can't. It's dangerous."

But Sister Emerenziana talks to my mother about it. In the end they give in. Who would possibly recognize me in that faraway part of the city so close to the fields and vegetable gardens?

Even though it's late in the day, I put on my black school uniform so I'll look more like one of those orphans you read about in books, and I follow the nun, staying very close behind her every step of the way.

I see shops that are almost empty, sidewalks with broken steps, people walking with their heads bowed.

But it's still the city, and for me it's like heaven.

When Mama came to live in the convent with us, the nuns had a little talk with me and my sisters.

"You're in a boarding school," they said, "and you have to behave like the other girls here. No trouble."

In other words, we can only go see our mother at six p.m. and for only one hour, and no more than that.

Every time, Mama rushes over to the farmers to buy an egg before we arrive.

Only one egg—you can't buy more than one, and if you do, they make you pay lots of money for them.

When Mama gets back to her room, she uses a spoon to beat that egg with sugar, until it becomes creamy. Then she uses the same spoon to feed us one at a time, like when we were little. We look like chicks that just hatched with their little beaks wide open.

One egg for three people: that's just one of the little tricks that war can play on you.

Hunger is the main topic at school.

Hunger is a terrible thing. You feel a squeezing

in your stomach, but you can't just say to yourself: *I think I'll have a snack now or maybe just a slice of bread.* There is no slice of bread, much less a snack! And you can hardly find anything else to eat, either.

Sometimes the nuns put frozen German potatoes on our plates. If we weren't so hungry, would we ever eat potatoes that taste so awful? They couldn't be any worse!

The nuns do have some food supplies in the cellar, but they can only be used a little at a time, otherwise they'll run out before the end of the war.

In the classroom we sing a song under our breath (but we sing it out loud in the hallways) to which we've changed the words. The words used to be "Oh lovely farm girl," but we've changed them to "Oh lovely plate of spaghetti." And we even changed the name of a great poet from the past from Ludovico *Ariosto* to Ludovico *Arrosto* (which means "roast").

I'm going to jump ahead a few months all the way to the spring (unfortunately, we were still at the boarding school) to tell you something wonderful.

Our nuns are called the Sisters of Saint Joseph, which means that they got their name from Saint Joseph.

So for them Saint Joseph's Day is the most wonderful feast day you can imagine.

On that day they call to us in their happiest voices, "Lunch is ready, girls! Come to the table!"

Talk about happy! We could faint, or start singing out for joy!

On the table in front of us are plate after plate of homemade spaghetti and sauce made with the tomatoes from our garden.

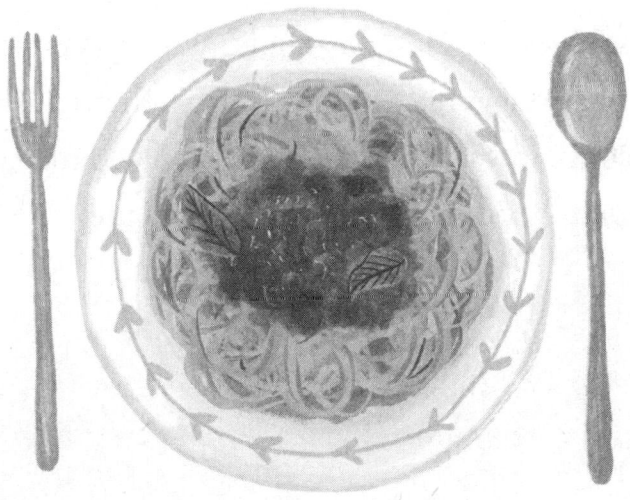

We can hardly believe our eyes, and almost reach out to touch the pasta just to make sure it's real.

But not only is it real—we can eat as much as we want! (Well, actually, soon there isn't any left.)

The nuns who did the cooking must have stayed up all night to prepare everything. But what about saving the food supplies? Well, for a feast day such as this, even the supplies can be used up.

Do you remember when I told you about the surprise dinner Nonna prepared for us with a view of the sea at sunset? I said that that was the most wonderful and unforgettable dinner I had ever had in my life.

I said *dinner*. Now I can add, without sounding like I'm exaggerating, that the spaghetti I ate at the convent was the most wonderful and memorable *lunch* I had ever had in my whole life.

14

PINA AND SPEPETTO

At boarding school I became friends with one of the other girls, and she's practically my best friend now.

Her name is Pina, she's Sicilian and, what's more important, she's brilliant.

She's a "prisoner" here at the boarding school like me, but only because the Americans landed in Sicily.

Right now, the Americans are fighting to liberate the rest of Italy (including us), but they're advancing very slowly, and for now there are "two Italys." Way down at the bottom are the ones who will come to save us, and farther up are the very evil Germans, who don't want to let them through.

Pina stays at school because she was a student here, and for now can't get back to her home in Sicily.

But she loves being here with the nuns. There's not a single thing they teach at school that Pina doesn't already know. Everyone admires her, but she never gives herself airs, not even a little.

She does something really nice for my sisters and me.

Many, many years ago, in the month of January, Mama and Papa got married, and on that exact day (which is the eighth) we would always celebrate their anniversary with a bouquet of flowers that Maria would buy for us.

But now our parents aren't even in the same place!

So this year we prepare a bouquet of flowers for them anyway. In the park we pick some white flowers called jonquils.

Pina looks at them and says, "They're beautiful,

but your father won't be able to see them. How can we let him know that we're thinking of him too?"

And that's when Pina starts writing a poem for their anniversary, which she is able to finish in just a few minutes. Mama will be able to bring the poem to Papa when they meet.

The poem goes like this:

*May these pure white jonquils
with their fragrance
express the love
of your three daughters.*

Le candide giunchiglie
possan con il loro odore
delle tre vostre figlie
esprimervi l'amore.

See how I remember it perfectly? Isn't it wonderful?

Mama tells us later that it made Papa cry.

There is one thing that really bothers me during these days.

When you're really good friends, you tell each other everything, right?

Pina and I talk about all kinds of things: the nuns—the nice ones and the ones who are not as nice—our other friends, some of whom are really silly (not like us), and also about our mothers and little sisters who are a nuisance (she has a little brother who stayed in Sicily with their parents and she's terribly jealous of him).

But I am keeping something very important from her.

I haven't told her I am Jewish (or even that my last name is fake—it isn't Lenti!).

But Papa made me swear that at boarding school I would never tell anyone I was a Jewish girl. And I absolutely have to keep my promise.

Papa said it's for our own safety.

But how can you talk about absolutely everything, and then hide something that is that important?

Every night, in bed, I think: *Tomorrow I'm going to tell her. I know I can trust her.* But then, that same night, I dream about my papa wagging his finger as if to say, *No! No!* And the next morning, I don't say anything.

In my head and in my heart I feel like our friendship is a little ruined.

Now, dear readers, I'm going to tell you something else that happened "afterward." When I was a grown-up, I met Pina in Sicily, and I found out that she knew I was Jewish the whole time! She had never mentioned it because she didn't want to upset me.

One day a terrible thing happens.

While Pina is playing, she falls off a wall and hurts her leg. The nuns think it would be a good idea to take her to the hospital to be sure nothing is broken.

While she's lying on the ambulance stretcher, Pina cries out, pointing at me, "I want her to come with me!"

The nuns exchange concerned glances, but then they decide, "Yes, let's make her happy. Poor girl, her parents are so far away!"

At the hospital, they take her to a dark room where a huge machine is pulled down from the ceiling so that, I think, they can take a picture of her bones.

Pina is so frightened she keeps squeezing my arm tighter and tighter.

I hold her hand as tightly as I can.

She thinks I'm doing it to keep her calm, but I'm clutching her because I'm more afraid than she is.

o o o

Spepetto on the other hand . . . I can't really call her a friend.

She's only three!

I already told you that lots of girls who were in danger came to the boarding school (especially that day it was raining when Mama came too).

The Germans haven't stopped. They keep looking for Jews in every house, and some families are on the run because they don't know where else to go.

At the boarding school there are parents who plead with the nuns to keep their girls: "Please, can you hide them?" The nuns always say yes, and another bed is added to our dormitory.

By now all the beds are so close to each other you can walk across as though they're one big floor.

But a three-year-old girl! So young she hasn't even been to nursery school yet! Girls that small couldn't possibly live at the boarding school.

Her mother kept insisting, even though the nuns

told her in no uncertain terms that there was absolutely no place for her daughter in the boarding house.

"All I ask is that you take my baby," she implored.

And can you guess what the nuns told her?

They said yes (it was the Mother Superior's decision).

What does a tiny little girl who's been left in a place where she doesn't know anyone do? She cries, right?

And to see her cry so much, we almost feel like crying too. The nuns don't cry—they can't—but sometimes they squeeze hands to give each other courage.

I remember that when my sister was three, I would pick her up, tell her stories, play little tricks on her to calm her down.

But that's not how things go with our small schoolmate. When she finally stops crying, we see what she's really like. Sometimes we can't see her at all, actually, because if you turn your back on her she will vanish suddenly. Then you see her again, climbing up some piece of furniture, hiding in between the chairs under the table, or running away so fast through the park—almost as far as the vegetable garden—that you can't catch up with her.

She pulls the nuns' veils and makes them crooked. And what about us girls? She whacks our pens and smudges our homework. Once, without any warning at all, she jumps into Sister Giacinta's arms and practically knocks her over. Sister Giacinta hugs her, but her eyes well up with tears.

All of us realize that no one in the little girl's family ever said no to her.

So it's the same at the school. If she wants something, she doesn't even think to *ask*. She simply raises her little finger and *gives an order*. And of course, everyone rushes to give her what she wants.

The nuns have never seen anyone like her in all their lives. At first, they are awestruck; then they start to be amused, like when you go to the cinema and see a funny movie.

Her real name is Rossana, but the sisters

nickname her Spepetto, which sounds like *pepe* (which means "pepper"). Why? Because everyone knows that pepper tickles your nose, but it also makes what you're eating taste better (although only grown-ups think that!).

A little bit of spice in the boarding school hallways isn't bad at all! It makes the boring things you have to do every day a little more exciting.

But one night, in the darkness of the dormitory, I hear what sounds like crying from her bed. It isn't the kind of sound she makes when she's acting up or crying because she skinned her knee. No. It sounds like she is crying into her pillow in secret, the way grown-ups do.

I walk over to her bed barefoot and look at her. Rossana, half asleep, with all those tears, must be dreaming about her mother.

Without making a sound, I pick her up and, even though I know it isn't allowed, take her to my bed.

I hug her, I stroke her hair, hoping the warmth